Also by Joseph E LeBlanc Jr

Oh Joe! A Father's Struggle to Survive the Loss of His Son
iUniverse, Inc.
1663 Liberty Drive
Bloomington, IN 47403
www.iuniverse.com

ISBN: 0-595-29666-1 (paperback)
ISBN: 0-595-66032-0 (cloth)

" … one of the most eloquent descriptions of grief that I have ever read. Mr. LeBlanc's book should take its place among those recommended for both professionals and students who wish to learn more about the intensity of parental grief and also for survivors of the death of a loved one (not necessarily parents) who wish the affirmation of a shared experience."

—Dr. Sharon B. Katz, grief counselor, Boise, Idaho, in
Bereavement—A Magazine of Hope and Healing, July/August 2004
edition

" … eloquently describes the process of grief and loss in a personal way … [A] must read for anyone who has lost someone dear to them."

—*The Unity Light*, a publication of the Unity Church of
Christianity, Houston, Texas, August 2004

" … moves through the broken-heartedness that characterizes parental bereavement. This book will sound familiar and be consoling to other bereaved parents as they, too, seek healing in the midst of profound loss."

—Rev. Paul A. Metzler, in *The Forum*, July/August/
September 2004 edition, a publication of the Association
for Death Education and Counseling

Defining Moments
Times and Happenings That Shape a Life
iUniverse, Inc.
1663 Liberty Drive
Bloomington, IN 47403
www.iuniverse.com

ISBN-13: 978-0-595-40413-1 (paperback)
ISBN-13: 978-0-595-84789-1 (cloth)

" ... *Defining Moments* presents a picture of a man's personal life with startling honesty and emotion. Joseph LeBlanc's slim volume is undoubtedly worth a read. ... Triumph and tragedy play out in the work, revealing the drama of everyday existence through poems that are simultaneously readable and remarkably introspective."

—*Forward* Clarion Reviews

"LeBlanc's collection of poems charts his development as a poet, husband, and father. ... It's a pleasure to read. ... Touching poetry about love, grief, and the ties that always bind."

—Kirkus Reviews

"Defining Moments is a more than a compilation of free-verse poetry; it is also the memoir and legacy of a devoted husband and father, spanning almost forty years. Author Joseph E. LeBlanc, Jr. offers a brief paragraph of context in preface to each poem; collectively, the verses reflect those moments of timeless memory, human choices, emotions, love, and inner conflict that shape life itself. Highly recommended."

—Midwest Book Review

THE ROAD IS ALWAYS FORKED

JOSEPH E. LEBLANC JR.

ROAD IS ALWAYS FORKED

iUniverse books may be ordered through booksellers or by contacting:

iUniverse
1663 Liberty Drive
Bloomington, IN 47403
www.iuniverse.com
1-800-Authors (1-800-288-4677)

ISBN: 978-1-5320-8688-5 (sc)
ISBN: 978-1-5320-8689-2 (hc)
ISBN: 978-1-5320-8687-8 (e)

Library of Congress Control Number: 2019917438

Print information available on the last page.

iUniverse rev. date: 01/10/2020

To my wife, Peggy, who famously observed, "You make choices, you pay prices, and you can't have it all."

As always, to my sons, Joe and Mark, for all they have given me and give me still.

And to life, that wondrous, rapturous experience that at once so engages and disowns us.

Contents

III. THEY SAID

IV. INWARD LOOKS

V. RANDOM THOUGHTS

Introduction

We learn early on that the road before us is forked. So begins the endless choices that we face. Mostly, we celebrate our freedom to choose until the choices are not so easy. How quickly we seek to turn them away. Who has not said—who has not heard—the plaintive cry, "I had no choice"? Which of us has not tried to force the decision upon another and let someone else take the blame? Who has not tried to wait it out, hoping that time will come to the rescue? Which of us has not deflected with the familiar refrain, "It's complicated"? But decisions will not be denied. They will be made by us whether by action or default. We choose even if we do not. Our choices spare us nothing. They follow us with their outcomes, the enduring legacy of what is done, the precursors of what is to come.

Chapter 1, "Choices," explores how we shy away from hard choices, trying to avoid the need to decide. There is no way out. We may not like the options or the consequences, but we always have a choice. Doing nothing is choosing as much as doing something. We are left with the aftermath just the same. Every decision leaves us different with what is added and what is taken and in the altered self that goes on.

These choices, the hard ones, come with a mix of feelings. Wistfulness at looking back. Wonder at what was done. Lament about what might have been. Temptation to second-guess. The regret of hindsight. And doubts that can haunt our choosing again, a hesitancy to act, an insistence upon a certainty not there, and the specter of failure. But choose we must, and we do as the cycle starts again.

I have come to a greater appreciation of how time weighs on our choosing and the changing perspective its passage leaves. Chapter 2, "Time Goes," reflects upon this added dimension. There is perhaps nothing that affects our choices more—the press of time, the limits of time, our measured time, knowing we will end, and the lessons and the burdens we take from the past. From it comes urgency, nostalgia, and angst about the future.

I write now from the perspective of having retired after forty-two years in the practice of law. I was often asked, "What will you do?" as if there were no more to me than my chosen profession. As I explained to a friend, the practice of law is what I did; it is not who I am. The best I could say then, and the best I can report now, is that I want to experience time differently, untethered to clock and calendar, unlinked from electronic devices and the phone, removed from deadlines and demands, absolved from the stress, feeling time as something to be savored and freely chosen. I have felt this need growing as there is a diminishing store of time ahead—even if its end seems abstract and far-off. It is more than just an awareness of time passing. It is the sensation of its going, of being lost for good. I asked myself, "How is it worthwhile to spend my remaining time?" Continuing what I was doing did not make the cut. There is more to my life. If anything else was to be done, it needed to be sooner rather than later.

We hear much talk about being in the moment. Are we ever not? We are forever fixed in an ongoing Now—each moment ethereal, instantly gone, consigned to the past, giving way to the next. I try to give voice to our being here and to the before and after moments that are the companions of Now, exerting their hold as baggage or harbinger, burden or hope. Time colors everything, leaving us to view forks in the road through the prism of the past, the lens of what lies ahead, and, more than anything, the knowledge of our inevitable ending.

We feel our way through this changing landscape, ever on the watch for signs to guide us. What informs our choices? What inspires us, spurs us to act, or frightens us into hiding? It can be anything, and in fact is many things. It may be a word here or there, a melody that catches our ear, a passing remark we hear for the first time, something newly seen or viewed in a new light, or aimless musings from which sudden epiphanies come. In Chapter 3, "They Said," I recount sources of inspiration that have found their way to me, with the hope that you too may look more closely at what has moved your life and moves you still.

They have emerged from the most common of places—words I have heard from others, lyrics of song, dialogue from movies, prose and poetry, sermons preached, and arguments engaged. They have all touched me in some way and moved me to greater insight into myself and my world—a nuance not thought of before or a thought long forgotten whose return is welcome. These sayings have called forth something that, but for them, might have been left undisturbed or unattended.

As we make our way, there is a tendency to ask, What does any of it mean? What does it matter? Where am I going? What became of the person I once was? The person I was going to become? Chapter 4, "Inward Looks," explores that inner place where we admit to these wonderings. I reflect on the self and how it has fared with the many claims upon it. This inner looking, if we will allow it, is a glimpse into the essence of us.

Finally, I have known the joy that comes from random thoughts—no choices to be made, no decisions at hand, just my mind taking me where it will. It is there we need to go, not to stay but for a while. Chapter 5, "Random Thoughts," turns to thoughts that have come to me on their own, freely floating without summons or direction; these are things I felt compelled to say without any need to do so. And so I have. There will be time enough to return to the demands of everyday. I must enjoy this respite while I can. This is the daydreaming of the child in us who has never left. What exciting days those were! And they can be again if we will let them. We daydream too little these days. We are told it is not efficient; it has no purpose. What is the point? But this is a part of us that needs tending, and we are less when we do not. How thankful I am to have preserved those set forth here.

The road ahead need not be as unsettling as it may seem. With a better understanding of our choices, with greater awareness of our place in time and how it affects our choosing, with a watchful eye and ear for the many inspirations that surround us, with deeper reflection upon ourselves and our world, and with our minds open to the random thoughts that come to us, we are better able to travel this road and, along the way, to experience life and time more intimately.

I. CHOICES

1.

We travel a road of our choosing. Things are asked of us we cannot foresee. Decisions must be made. Was it the wrong choice? Should I have done something different? Who has not said this? Whose thoughts have not gone there? We write a story yet to be told, its narrative formed by what is done and what is left behind. Would the choices not made have been better? Who knows? We are where we are and must do with what we have done. And always there is the next choice to be made.

The Road Ahead

Open road ahead,
uncharted,
even if traveled by others,
not yet mapped by me.
Where will my goings take me?
Best-laid plans have their limits,
yielding to choices this way or that,
not knowing where until there,
then to measure how close
to what I chose
or thought I did.

Is it blessing or curse
not to see round the bend?
Blessing or curse to choose?
To whom will I surrender
the plotting of my way?
My wilderness is not yours.

Thanks are due that I can set my life,
the mistakes mine.
Shifting blame always returns—
how else would I learn?
Choices have brought me here;
next steps lead me where,
nearer to what I see
or wandered off?

I give as much shape as I can.
For every fall, ascent,
for every missed turn,
a chance to correct,
best efforts,
best guesses,
all I have.
This is my world,
I would choose no other.

—October 2014

2.

Choices are freighted with their own anxiety, not knowing what's best, the prospect of mistake always there. It colors our thinking. What if we fail not just ourselves? What if we cause pain or hurt if we are wrong or even right? If loss is suffered, who should bear it? The thought of doing nothing may be tempting. It is a choice nonetheless. It holds us in place and allows what happens. We are not victims of what comes. We may have reckoned it the lesser of two evils, and we less culpable, but it is no less our doing.

Choices Made ... Choices Not

Choices,
the hard ones,
can overcome with the menace
of what they hide,
downsides everywhere,
none fair or fine,
but closing fast,
unseen, unknown,
but not unfelt.

How we fear their coming,
shrink from their making
as if we can elude their reach,
as if Time would take them back.
But they survive our not doing,
deciding for us if they must,
leaving us with a shaken world
we claim was forced upon us.

What delusion!
Its coming was not without warning,
nor we the unwitting victim.
What was wrought was the reason
we would not choose;
our choice unmade delivered it here.

Time with its demands will not be put off;
tomorrow never comes until it does;
each day's beginning or end,
the hand is ours.
Time will not save us from ourselves.

Our choices outlive their making,
sometimes their maker,
with what they take and leave,
evidence they have been here,
but enough sweetness,
enough light
to keep us going,
or so we hope
until this too is taken,
nothing left.

—August 2006

3.

Choices carry a cost. Much can hang in the balance. Much does when choices are summed up. They are the unhappened future before it has arrived, offering us a say in what will be. There is weight to what we do. We cannot have it all. What price are we willing to pay? We must weigh the best we can and then choose. A price will be paid whatever we do.

Prices Paid

It is done.
I have chosen,
or not.
No matter, it is the same,
and now the reaper comes calling
with gifts of reward or remorse,
failings or blessings,
before moving on.

How much of the choosing was mine?
So much to take into account,
so many others,
not just me.
Did I have a choice or
am I at some other's whim?
Why does Time toy with me so,
unwilling to slow or give me more?
Why must it be now?
If I do not choose, am I free?
Am I victim
or did it have my favor?

It is not the choices we fear
but their portents and omens.
Will it be as good or bad as that?
Tempted to wait and see,
they will not steer clear,
give us no berth
until they wash over us,
leaving a world always of our choosing
whether we did or not.

—July 2015

4.

"I had no choice." How often have we said this? How often have we heard it? It is a weak defense. Downsides do not mean we could not choose. We weighed the outcomes. Was the cost too great? Was the benefit too little? Which way would the loss or hurt be greater or less? There may have been no good answer. But we chose—we did something or nothing. We picked one and must live with it.

No Choice

Choices,
when they come,
do not arrive alone,
their sequel not far behind
with the fearsome threat of what
they will deliver—
or, worse, that the hand was ours,
the weighing the last refuge
before it happens,
this safe place soon swept up
in Time's roll,
the plaintive cry of "no choice"
now a feeble echo with no purchase,
dread of what lay ahead now moot.

There were downsides to them all
as we struggled,
desperate to measure living with,
living without,
unable to know until revealed,
and we left to ask,
What if I had gone the other way?

How to choose in this conflicted world?
How to survive what cannot be undone?
Here lies the fear,
not of the choosing
but the damage that may come.
And here lies the hope,
always in next choices
until there are none.

—August 2006

5.

No one has it all despite much talk of it. Some seem to have it, though no one claims it for themselves. There is no *all* to be had—always something more to acquire, more to gain, always someone better off, someone left behind. Perhaps having it all simply means having more, but how much more? And what of the cost to get there? Prices are paid by each of us in singular ways, often beneath the surface. No one gets through life unscathed. Life is not easy for anyone. Forget the outward appearances. The pretense and façade are for our benefit. The ravages of life are there in the shadows.

Having It All

How can you have so much?
How can your life be that good?
Why do you not struggle
like the rest?
You have it all.

Do not look too closely.
Just below are the sufferings
going by different names,
cleaned up,
sanitized,
passing as something else,
still there,
afflictions and sadness,
loneliness and loss,
on display or not,
visible or kept under wraps.
No one is unwounded,
no escape from life's random.

How many unseen drownings
are in full sight?

Something must give.
There is a limit to winning hands
and winners;
only the faces change.
We each pay a price.

—July 2015

6.

We put off decisions if we can. There is hope for more clarity with time when the choices will somehow be easier. Does later have such power? How long shall we wait? The burden of choosing can be disheartening, with endless mulling of options and wondering, "What if?" If we hold out for certainty, we are doomed. It is rare in this world. We can only decide as best we can and not let life pass us by.

Fences

We sit on fences all life long,
daunted by choices,
everywhere to turn.
Which way? Why?
Such freedom,
so abandoned,
the specter of mistake so freezing.
What if this? What if that?

And so we wait for a clarity
that never comes,
the choice rarely clearer,
often worse for the endless dally,
as one day turns into the next,
with us poised on fences of
our making,
pretending to struggle with the choice
with no advance,

waiting for someone to help us down
if we will let them,
until Time takes over and
it is moot.

—May 2001

7.

We are set in our ways more than we may think. How early did the setting begin? If too soon, we exclude much of life and its possibilities. We risk contracting our world too much. The seeming comfort of nothing changing is a poor exchange for choices open to us. They can be awakening and energizing. We must leave room for the new and the different, not leave to others the marvels to come that might have been ours.

Set in Our Ways

Looking back,
have we been set in our ways
too long?
Did we become set
too soon?
How much of life has passed us by
because not let in,
our world narrowed into seeming safety?

What was so fearful,
so threatening, it was not worth
a chance?
How much did we exclude
as not worth the effort for reasons
that no longer matter,
are no longer remembered?

Now that time has passed,
are we left to wonder:
How much?
For what?
Is there time left?

—February 1999

8.

Hindsight can rob the present and prey upon the future. Most times, there is much to be thankful for from our choices—at least something. Other times, hindsight can render a harsh judgment. Even that must be kept in perspective. It assumes other choices would have been better, often with no way to know. Change anything and you change everything. There is no way to say any conjured outcome would have been that way. Too much intervenes. We should not be so quick to trade our presence here with regret for not being somewhere else. We cannot know where that would have been. Instead, we should see hindsight as a wise teacher leading us to better choices ahead.

Hindsight

Hindsight,
you have an easy life,
looking back with that unforgiving eye,
faulting us with illusions of better,
assurances never tested by time or life.
You could make them anything,
your hand never called,
leaving us with sentences of doubt and guilt
for choices we would take back
if we knew then
what you show us now was true,
when even you could not know sooner.
All you have is an un-moment
that never was,
what next beyond even you.

Hard as you are on us,
we and our choices move on
until you try again,
our only defense it was the best
we could do,
or so we tell ourselves,
until we believe or no longer know,
or someone says different,
the question always close at hand.
It is easy looking back from now
when it is over.
So clear, you say.
Why did we not see?

There is much to like
where my choices have brought me,
much I would not trade,
your reproach the only way here
or I would be somewhere else.
Better? Worse? Who can say?
I'll take here.

—September 2014

9.

Regret and its twin, guilt, loom large when we are wrong about the big things, sometimes even the small. Once arrived, they are here to stay, try as we might to ignore them. We learn to make an uneasy truce. For all the pain, there is comfort to be found. We hurt because we care. We learn lessons not to be acquired any other way. Regret is often the price to grow, guilt the cost to prevent repeat.

Regret

Regret exacts a dreadful toll,
arrived unbidden,
its grip will not ease,
nothing enough to elude its reach
or the guilt wedded to it.
Forgiveness can only do so much;
memory has taken hold of
what cannot be undone,
what wishing cannot make right,
what need not make sense.

Regret,
Have you no mercy?
Have you no heart?
You are a callous jailer,
the sentence never served,
kept in solitary.
What more do you want?

Or Regret,
Are you more generous than you seem,
warning against doing again?

Is this your work after all,
warding off same mistakes,
more caring than you seem
as we labor to make peace
with you?

—February 2006

10.

The fear of mistake can check us in our tracks, hoping the moment will pass without having to choose. Better yet, perhaps someone else will decide. At least the mistake will not be ours, or so we tell ourselves. But we cannot outrun the choices facing us. Our turn will come. We must take the risk of failing for the chance of succeeding. Life is more than doing as little as possible to avoid being wrong. It is made of leaps of faith and chance. If a mistake is made, at least it will not be because we did not try. We will not be at the mercy of someone else's wrong.

The Fear of Mistake

What if we are wrong?
The weight of brewing blame
forces its way into our thinking,
seizing more as the stakes rise.
It will not be banished,
cannot be reasoned away,
no going back before it appeared,
as we, desperate to avoid,
weigh the safety of delay.

We cannot walk away so easily;
the choices will not have it,
willing to settle for nothing from us,
leaving to them what is forced upon us,
with we still in the chain
for we let them in,
gave them free hand,
no protest,
it was surrendered too,

no one else to blame for what
we would not stop.

Act! Act! We must!
At least then the mistake
if it comes
will not find us in hiding,
triumphed over without a fight,
our best unused,
never tried,
never tested,
never having to be overcome.

—September 2014

11.

"She said a bad day is when I lie in the bed and I think of things that might have been," sang Paul Simon in "Slip Sliding Away." However much we may wonder, we are unfair to ourselves if we allow this thinking to diminish what we have now. There is no way to know what might have been. There are too many unknowns, too many intersections, too many forks in too many roads to assume anything else would have been. Life would have intervened in different choices in unknowable ways just the same. If something else could have been, it would have been. Even so, we find it hard to avoid these musings. Other paths may have been better. But they may have been worse. There is no "what if" world so certain we can say we have been denied or missed out. We lessen our present and saddle our future to think there is. All we have is the world we have made and the one to come that awaits our next choices.

What Might Have Been

How we long for the times
that never were,
other lives we are sure
would have unfolded just
as we dreamed,
what might have been,
taken by death too soon,
lost by answers that no longer measure up,
abandoned on roads not taken,
put off when their only time was then,
waiting for a second chance when
there was only one,
the hope to choose again when

they, like me,
passed this way only once.

What an illusion!
Whatever life the not chosen
might have had
is gone with never was,
its chances over,
its time passed.
So let me take nothing from
my time now and to come
in anguished wondering,
in moonstruck pining
for something that never was,
something that if it could have been
would have been.

—August 2015

12.

We hear much about being the best as if nothing else will do. This is certainly the goal. But everyone cannot be the best. And rarely can one thing be singled out as the best. The fact is, the world does not require the best. It could not go on if it did. Most times, efforts need only be good enough. Many times, the best may not be sought at all. Evidence of this abounds. Who has not witnessed a job performance that could be done better? Who has not seen an employment position filled by someone not up to the task, the Peter Principle the only limit and sometimes not even then? Who has not observed the favored few supplanting merit? How much better and best goes unused?

The Rule of Enough

The world turns round based upon
a rule of enough,
the best lauded as a goal,
lofty heights at times achieved,
and should be if within reach,
but most often not,
and the world goes on without it,
so long as the effort is enough for
what must be done,
the least required winning out.

This is no tribute to not trying,
no call for acceptance of less.
Far more, it is a hailing of the world
as it is,
where good enough can be
all that is needed,
all that is wanted,

enough to get by,
enough to not leave undone,
enough to not do too poorly,
not slighted for not being the best,
if there is such a thing
in an infinite world,
where lines blur between better and better,
each vying for the top,
no way to decide,
ever changing,
while good enough soldiers on.

—March 2008

13.

Life rarely turns out exactly as we planned. Too much is unforeseen, too much beyond our control. How do we handle the shortfall? When are dreams gone for good? When do we know? What takes their place? What we do next determines everything. There need not be only one dream. The unknown holds out the promise of more. Success? Failure? Do not presume before the effort is made. Hurdles ahead might be pushed through more easily than you think. Do not be left—do not leave—with never knowing.

The Shortfall

It is not coming,
the future I envisioned.
Another has arrived in its place,
waiting turned to delusion at last,
no question of want or effort more,
it is here.

Do I make it less with my discontent
or explore its realms,
open to what it offers,
not sullen over what I have lost?
I must take the world as I find it,
as it has found me,
offering another chance
to make the most.

I cannot lament forever.
Better to turn and face,
embrace,
and carry on.
There is new planning to do.

—March 2016

14.

Difficult decisions confront us with what we can live with and what we cannot live without. Change may seem the only answer, if for no other reason than we have no other answer. But change has its price. Our history can burden the peace we seek. We must be aware of this and make it part of our choosing. Was it right or wrong? Was it worth it? Hard questions, the answer often not known until later.

Living With … Living Without

What can you live with?
What can you not live without?
You cannot know until looking back,
for all the certainty of what you must have,
it is not so simple.
As much as you see,
as much as you take into account,
there are hidden costs.

When you weigh what you must have,
regard too what you leave behind,
it will not go gently;
you will feel it still a part of you.
How much will it take
from what you cannot live without?
Will the golden days urging you on
appear?
Will the hellish days you flee
be gone for good?
Will there be enough left
for your gamble?

Be ready to live with what you choose,
knowing what you must have
and what you can no longer abide
play against each other.

Happiness,
will you be forever cheated?
Or is that you approaching,
your vigil over?

—August 2014

15.

We often think of things as over and done with, even as we recognize that the past is always with us. In the movie *Alice Adams*, Katherine Hepburn declared, "Oh, everything's over *some* time, isn't it?" William Faulkner, in his novel *Requiem for a Nun,* differently observed, "The past is never dead. It's not even past." Both speak truths. How much of the past is gone and has nothing more to say, and what continues to lay claim to us? The past has a mind and voice of its own. We will hear from it and must contend with it.

Over and Done With

Past,
are you ever over and done with,
or have you never left,
finding a new place and willing ears
for your lessons?
We delude ourselves to think
we can leave behind what we wish,
carry forward what we will
as if we were the sole judge
dispensing a future of our making.

The Past will always have a say
and exact a charge
as long as it commands our attention,
unwilling to release memories
we least want,
deflecting our efforts to suppress,
stoking what we wish to dispel,
reminding us of wrongs done and
paths not taken,

other times welcome if we agree,
leading us onward, upward
to heights we have been to once
and will go again,
pointing the way to summits
we aspire to from afar.

It is a mixed blessing,
the Past,
not ever fully over and done with,
not ever finally done with us.

—December 2007

16.

How often do we tell ourselves we are making an accommodation only "for now" and until a mythic "then"? Just a temporary concession for larger goals. We will make amends with ourselves later. But "for now" has a way of not ending and "then" has a way of never coming. We all have something of the Faustian bargainer as we trade away parts of us with little sacrifices here, small compromises there, so sure time will keep us in check—we will right the ship then. We should not wait too long.

For Now ... Until Then

How we play with time
to suit our ends,
using it to barter for what we want,
"for now" a way to bargain,
"until then" a way to take it back,
to save us from our undoing,
to live to trade again,
sure we could say when,
when to start,
when to stop.
We could always come back.

Time does not go so gently,
its measure more than us.
We may find
after taking what we want,
after dealing knowing better,
after counting our winnings,
when we turn back
there is no land in sight.

We have ventured too far,
"for now" lasted too long,
"then" has been reclaimed by Time,
and what was put aside
is gone for good.

Are we there yet?
Is "then" still on the way?
If we act now,
will it be soon enough?

—November 2011

17.

Do we each have a tipping point of no more trade-offs to get ahead, no more set-asides of self to get along? The surrenders may seem small until they add up, or there is so little time left they are all there is. Is there a point where we say, "Enough"? Where is the line drawn? It differs for each of us and changes with age.

The Tipping Point

We have limits to how far we can stray
from selves that will not be turned away,
the leaving in small steps at first,
covering more ground than we knew,
more than we wanted to know,
until we looked back
or felt the distance.

How to know when
we have gone too far?
The line moves with us,
with stealth so we hardly notice;
it will last forever if we let it,
leading to places we would not choose.
What is my tipping point?
What is yours?
Is it here?
Is it now?

It is hard,
this turning back,
returning to those who knew us first
and knew us well,

lead by small rememberings
and a growing feel of home,
not shedding new friends made
along the way;
they are welcome to come.
I hope they do.

—September 2014

18.

We live in a culture that insatiably asks for more. We cannot leave; it is where we are. It draws us in slowly. Then bigger moves as the promise of better and more takes hold. Warnings and reproaches of others have little sway. They do not understand. We are convincing to ourselves. We bond with the world we have entered. It has a place for us, shows every sign of welcome, but always ready to discard. It takes what it can, as the world outside offers less or not enough to prompt our return. How do we break free? Only we can start the journey back to once familiar ground.

Stockholm

How enticing our captors are!
We know many by name:
Ambition, Success, Acclaim.
How easy it is to fall under their spell!
They do not ask too much too soon,
but hold out enough not to walk away
without sampling more,
until there is no way to leave
without losing what brought us there,
and we, not ready for that,
will leave later.

Their promise cannot last,
offering only more of the same,
nameless faces ready to take our places,
it is all the same to them,
peddlers to whomever will have them,
no care for my life or yours.

Looking back
to where we began,
at who we would choose to be,
are we ready to return?
Not all at once,
in small steps as we left.
Do we know the way?
What arms will greet us?
They have their captors too.

—October 2014

II. TIME GOES

19.

What is time? We are aware of it in relation to us, but otherwise do not give it much thought. Most of us do not think of it in terms of relativity, or as bended or folded, or whether it is limited by the speed of light. This is not needed to go about our days. We may never turn our attention to these abstractions. I tend to think of time something like this—at least for now.

Time

Time is existence,
the absence of nothingness
or ending,
independent of all else,
needing nothing, no one,
going on alone,
silent, dark.
It is itself.

It is ours too,
but only a small slice,
our consciousness its domain,
our life its limit.
We measure it,

name it:
Past, Present, Future,
Sooner, Later,
Now, Then,
Come, Gone.

We track ourselves in it,
call it aging,
mark our beginning and ending,
witness our moving through it,
our panic at its going,
departing with us then,
all of it we ever had
as if we never had.

How we took it for granted
when it was here
and treasured it
whether we knew it
or not.

—April 2019

20.

Nothing defines time for us more than knowing we will end and not knowing when. We count our place on a continuum of unknown distance. We record the past because it was here. We were there. We plan for the future because we have not yet ended. We will speak of it until we are. Perhaps it is a blessing that we do not know.

Time and Us

Time,
what a solitary companion you are!
Mine alone for me,
my measure of you is not yours,
your counting of me as far removed
from others,
we share what we can.

What a chilling spell is cast
knowing we will end,
not knowing when,
wondering if the time is now
or soon,
rushing us to force what living we can,
or giving up or slowed,
fearing signs of its approach.
What is the point?

But let us suffer no ending before its time
or so little effort we are as well gone.
Time is the jealous guardian of its run,
not to be calendared by lesser souls,
we the master of what we can

before it is taken,
with all the angst
of waiting until then.

—August 2014

21.

When I retired from the practice of law, I was asked, "What will you do?" I felt no need to account for what would come. The best I could say was that I wanted to experience time differently—without the demands of clock and calendar, court deadlines and client timetables. To do what I want. To do nothing if I choose. And so I have. I have reclaimed time. I can feel it, sense it, be immersed in it. The sensation is palpable. The days, the hours are mine. We tend to commoditize time, to view it as something to be filled and wasted if it is not. Little value is seen in unfilled time, independent of doing, to be savored without regard for effort or return. This is too often not appreciated, too often delayed, too often never felt. And then time runs out.

Experiencing Time Differently

Time comes at us in different ways,
its power least with its limits far off,
but growing as it closes in,
and we forever changed knowing
it is coming.

It can consume every moment
when there are too few,
can unnerve us when unfilled,
can leave us in wide-eyed dismay when
there are no claims upon us.
We are on our own.

Time ages with us,
easing its demands
as it continues its retreat,
no longer the hard taskmaster,

now standing in wait as we approach,
felt as not before,
something going,
something to lose,
everything we know.

You are mine at last,
not missed this much before now.
I can feel you,
fill you,
sense your flow at my hand.
Everything takes on new meaning,
details show themselves
there all along.
I am author,
I am actor,
waiting for Time to say when.

—December 2013

22.

I cannot write of time without mention of the "time sheets", the curse of defense lawyers everywhere who must account for each hour because they're paid based upon hours billed. A record required for each day. It is one thing to be aware, abstractly, that time is passing. It is quite another to register its going in print, there to see in black and white. Day after day. Case after case. Arguments and positions repeat themselves, only the names changing. This mattered little in the beginning, other than the tedium of the writing. But as my time left grows less, remaining time becomes more urgent and more real. What is a worthwhile way to spend it? There will always be more work. Another time sheet. Is this all I have left to do with the rest of my life? I asked these questions. And then I retired. It felt right. It was time. There is more to me than this. I have never looked back.

The Time Sheets

Mere sheets of paper to be filled out,
or were they?
Perhaps in the beginning,
but how ominous they became,
a diary of fleeting time
certified by my hand without a blink,
witness, epitaph, of a passing life
with less of me in it,
more signed away with each stroke
as Joe Black comes closer.

Is this what I have come to?
More of the same,
written descriptions with no content
beyond the writing,

no value beyond the currency of payment
that could be for anything?
There is more to me than what
the time sheets say.

More or Other would come later,
I argued to myself,
but they never do on their own;
they must be summoned.
And so I called and Later came,
Other too.
I am free,
released from the weight and the summary
that miss so much about me.

What will I do?
Not this,
not any longer.
No more days disappeared into the writing,
my reclaimed time newly at my beck,
and yet the time sheets, though put away,
their ghost remains,
ever the reminder of life come and gone
and going.

—July 2014

23.

We are told to be "in the moment." Are we ever not? We live in an ongoing Now, not leaving with moments when they pass, not able to join ones to come before they are here. What do we make of the moment when we have it? Do we fill it with action and purpose? At least awareness and appreciation? Do we let it pass as nothing special, as if there is no limit to how many more? Do we wish it away, dwelling upon an embellished past or fantasizing a romanticized future? How easily we can be seduced to trade the moment Now for one of them. And yet the moment is not without them. It includes the past as the sum of what has gone before and the future from the plans made for its coming. The one informs with lessons learned, the other to be taken into account so long as we are here. The challenge is to not let them draw us too far from the present moment, rendering it less than it could be. We owe all we have to our moments and to the person we will become.

In the Moment

What an effort it is to stay
in the moment,
resisting the safety of the past
because it is over,
the appeal of a future able to promise
anything because it is not here,
tempting us to wait for better times,
sure they are ahead,
or mourning them gone.
Better is an easy sell when not yet lived
and generous when not needing
to be lived again.

Moments do not arrive alone,
weighed down with baggage and worry,
anxious anticipation or wistful looking,
millstones upon Now,
and we, stunted,
flee to Past or Future
for the comfort of not this.

The moment is there for salvage
if we will feel its openness to us,
fill it with our joy of it,
suffused within it,
stealing none of our presence from it,
aware there is none like it and,
unknown to us,
may be no more,
wondering
if we made the most of the past
when it was here,
planned best for the future
if it appears, and
if what we give our moment Now
will bring better ones to come.

—March 2010

24.

Our efforts to remain in the moment can only do so much. The enticement of the past and the ease of wishing for the future can lure us away. We may find ourselves lingering in memories that cannot be called back or in reverie for what has yet to come and may never be. Why is it so hard to resist? Only the present has something to give. How much do we miss because we are not here?

Time Travel

We travel in time,
though not thought of that way,
longing for a Past that cannot
get worse,
at risk no longer,
holding out for a Future
not yet judged,
not yet here,
hopeless romantics.

How can Now compete
with hands never called,
allure never lessened?
They cannot fall short,
cannot disappoint,
need deliver nothing,
do no more than take from Now,
leaving us with moments lost
or less than might have been
had we given them a chance.

We can travel only so far
from Now,
its event horizon holding us here.
We must fill it to its crest
while in our hands,
forcing if we must,
for it will not stay
and must not leave empty
of us.

—May 2007

25.

It is the little things that are lost in the shuffle of life. More is demanded than can be done at once. Something has to give. Something has to wait. We assume there will be time for these less pressing matters, that their day will come, until it does not. And so is gone more of the little things. Put off forever. Perhaps it cannot be any other way. We cannot do it all. Still, let us not lose sight of these lesser things. They have much to add to life if we will spare them the time.

The Little Things

Little things are missed
under the press of larger claims
consumed with the urgency of now,
finer details of life passed by,
taken for granted,
not intended to be ignored,
more not noticed,
their cries not as loud.

Undone,
they do not slow the pace of life,
patiently wait their turn
until Time releases them to us
if they are still there,
now ready for the savoring,
the simple awe of them,

or lament if Time took them back,
not known until nowhere to be found,
no memory of what we never knew,
only too late it is gone.

—January 2014

26.

How well do we handle time on our hands? At some point, the demands upon us lessen. More of our time is ours. The feeling can be unnerving. There is a void, a pressure to do something, anything rather than nothing. But why? What has such power over us? We have moments to spend as we choose, and there is no rush. There is much to discover in this newly-returned time.

Time Freed

Our time is consumed
in the roles we are cast,
forced upon us or of our choosing,
seeming right at the time
until it is returned to us.
Phone silenced, no one calling,
calendar empty unless we write,
our comings and goings not demanded,
not required, not even known,
up to us to venture forth.

Time unfilled can overwhelm
with demands for attention.
What to do with no one to tell me,
no one to ask of me?
Where to go if I must not be anywhere?
When to do anything if there is no clock?
To whom do I matter if no one is here?
What interests me with no one insisting?

For some,
an uncharted world to explore,
the unknown concealing new selves.
For others,
a return to familiar ground or
pursuit of a wish seen from afar.
For all,
the excitement and relief
of nothing to prove,
time freed the only way there.
What will you find?
Who will you be?

—June 2010

27.

In the movie *While We're Young*, Ben Stiller wistfully remarks to Naomi Watts, "I'm forty-four and there are things I will never do. Things I won't have." We are all there at some point, recognizing there are things we planned that we will no longer do. The reasons are many. Life is a series of trade-offs. Choices have to be made. Time has its boundaries. We know this. Still, the fact of "never doing" brings its own sadness.

Time Takes

We start
with the best of intentions,
hopes and dreams
with a lifetime to reach,
more than enough time;
we'll figure it out.

Then the putting off begins,
the reasons not at fault.
Time has its own order
and takes not with malice
but matter-of-fact with its passing,
reeling us in with its limits
even while our eyes still see more,
dreams outgrown, aged out,
ever further out of reach.

Not all is lost.
There are laurels on which to rest;
new vistas come into view;
new dreams are born,

closer at hand,
more suited to now,
a tenuous compromise with Time,
urging us on
until Time's next taking,
until Time's last.

—July 2017

28.

We speak of time as wasted, but it is more than achievement alone, more than winning or losing, making progress or falling behind. It is not without worth if it is none of these. Even if unfilled for the moment or fallen short in the effort, it affirms much about us, proof of our presence and evidence of the choices that brought us here. Our time has value because we have value. It is the sum of us.

Time Wasted

We fill time with parts of us,
never all,
never wasted while we are in it,
filling it with what we could
or would;
it is what we needed then.

Hindsight, Regret,
you cannot take this from us.
We were there
with our triumphs and rejoicing,
our heartbreaks and defeats,
what was called for in the moment,
or so we thought,
not to be written off as lost;
there was no other road to here.

Time leads us on to fill again,
the best in us still here,
waiting,
waiting for another chance
to get it right,

to get it better,
to fill it more,
if Time will give it
and will we.

—March 2019

29.

We are urged to share our feelings but do so only so much. There are things we feel alone. We can describe them, but even this falls short. At times we may not know what we feel, aware only of symptoms that disturb and disrupt. We may not be able to identify—or be ready to admit—why we feel as we do, encountering defenses hard to surmount. Others face this too as we turn to each other and try our best to understand.

The Felt Things

We are alone with the felt things,
what we alone can feel,
often not knowing what it is
or why,
just that all is not well.

They are not to be dismissed lightly,
these felt things.
They come from somewhere,
are not without their reason,
tell us something,
sometimes defying our attempts
to name them,
sometimes named more benign,
denial is less painful.
Unable to be turned away,
they must be faced,
ignored, unheeded at our peril.

They are possessive of us,
found nowhere else,
can be shared only so much.
Others can describe what they see,
tell what they hear,
sympathize, console,
empathize if they have been there
or close enough,
doing the best they can,
but there are hurts
they cannot know,
bound in their own felt world
as far removed from me.
It helps that they are here.
Do I help them too?

—January 2014

30.

"I'm bored." How often have we heard this? How many times said it? What does it mean? Not that there is nothing to occupy our time, for there clearly is. Where is the inquiring mind curious about what it does not know? Where is the interest in trying something different? In learning something new? Where is the desire to help someone in need? You will not have to look far. At times this has no appeal. We would as soon do nothing, waiting instead for something to distract or entertain. This is an opting out of time, a failing to appreciate the moment for the fact that we have it and cannot know how many more. We should make use of it if in no other way than to be thankful it is here. In "Secret, O Life," James Taylor sang, "The secret of life is enjoying the passage of time." Perhaps this is it.

Boredom

Life and Time
do not allow for boredom,
the flux of them,
the imaginings of each moment,
the choices forced upon us,
the feelings wrenched from us,
the callings reached out to us
will not be ignored.

We should feel each moment
before it is gone,
unique,
none like it,
no chance to feel it again.
How many moments have we let
slip away unloved,

unwanted,
not worth the effort,
when Time was so generous
to give them to us?

—August 2015

31.

As more of life is lived, we may ask, What's left? What untapped potential? What next levels to reach? Or is the subject never broached, as if we are left with only what has been done? Time has not been given to remain unused and unexplored. There is more to do so long as Time will allow.

My Heart Beats Still

Years unfold
and we travel with them—
into what?
What potential remains unmined?
What chances have perished from neglect?
What wonders are but a moment away?

My heart beats still,
reminding me there is more to come,
more to be drawn from me.
I must search.
I must create.
The unknown not to be feared;
it excites and whets,
or should.

My soul stirs at the thought.
I am ready.
Come to me, Time,
in a rush or slowly
as you wish.
Past,
be not impatient,

I will be there soon enough.
Future,
I am waiting.
Ending,
where are you?
How close have you come?
Are you even now within my reach?

—December 2015

32.

We are many selves during our lives. We grow older. New people, old people, move in and out of our lives. Our choices change. Decisions alter our landscape. The decades bring new challenges, new perspectives. Responsibilities and demands differ. We have new wants and value other things. Is it drawing from us different selves never meant to stay? Does each build upon the next, adding and discarding what is needed or not? And what of our departed selves? Are they ever truly gone?

Many Selves

How Time toys with who
we are!
Past wars with Present,
Future in the balance,
Present with the edge if we will let it,
creating new Pasts before they join
the gone befores,
the world at our hand,
always becoming who will become,
then taking its place with who we were,
Time drawing different selves from
where we are.

Were they always to be found,
these other selves,
formed and waiting?
Or were they formed anew for
what was needed,
new births demanded by the moment
for as long as it lasts?

And then
as Time asks less,
are old selves left behind,
their time passed?
Are future selves in wait,
not knowing if their day will come
or if we have treated them well?

Until Time tires of the game,
and we,
alone at last,
glimpse who we are with all else
gone.

My selves,
once so firmly in my grasp,
now all turns to liquid
as it slips away.

—September 2016

33.

I find these days that I sometimes get maudlin. Not for too long. Not so much dwelling on what has gone before as more aware. I reflect more on the past because there is now more of it, growing larger as more accumulates and smaller as memories go, a paradox of time. Memories have greater impact even as they grow dimmer. Some stand out with the same clarity as when they occurred. I look at them all, weighing how I have done. Do I judge I could have done better? Or take my winnings, my losing, as my best at the time? It cannot be done again. I've had my chance. Small wonder that I sometimes feel maudlin.

Maudlin

The Past comes at me
in new ways now,
reaching deeper
as I contend with the weight
of what is gone,
what will never be,
as the knowns take their leave
and the unknowns loom large,
what has been lived,
what has been survived,
the fading and the knowing,
felt again but differently now
and changing,
the history and the memories
that can bring tears.

Have I done all I could?
Have I left too much unfinished,

too much behind,
the silent victim of too late,
the undone felt like a limb taken off
or how they say it would feel?

The joys of roads taken remain,
still alive in how they move me,
and in the hope
that spirits kindred to them
even now are on their way,
to be celebrated or mourned
like all the rest.

—July 2016

34.

Time has a way of releasing tears that have gathered unshed. Much of our lives are spent with a game face on, tears not a luxury. They can be rallied in times of pain and loss and sorrow; emotions alone would be too much. And so they collect, waiting for Time's loosening. Perhaps we would all cry more easily if not trying so hard not to.

I Cry

I cry more easily now
as a lifetime of emotion is pushed
to the fore by memory and loss,
mine
and those close to me
and those I do not know,
accumulations of life steeled against
to get by,
to get through,
but never gone.
Where would they go?

Called forth by new beginnings
all around,
no longer mine,
how I wish them well
through the unknowns to come.
I have been there,
have made it through;
they can too.

Summoned again by endings
too close for comfort,
as another and another are gone
that knew the world I know,
all of us on a road never wanting
to travel alone,
knowing one of us must.

—October 2018

III. THEY SAID

35.

"I like crowds because they are anonymous," a friend once said. I was struck by the comment. Anonymity can have this appeal. No demands. No one looking. Nothing expected. Nothing to live up to. There is refuge there, however temporary and tenuous. How widespread is this appeal?

The Crowd

In ones and twos
your numbers swell about me
until I am no longer me
but one of you,
my deserted face
reappeared in your varied expression,
my trembling limbs
lost among your undirected heaves.
Within your refuge
I cannot be found.
I am secure, impregnable,
so long as you will have me,
rid of all remorse,
for my want is not my own.
And then
as suddenly as you became,

in ones and twos you remove,
no further thought of me or you,
a derelict with no mind, no care,
only to arise again
indifferent to it all.

—February 1974

36.

How I like to read! How I like discourse with another who likes to read! And so it was one day, during talk of Jane Austen and Daphne du Maurier, that one of my nieces remarked, "I like a well-turned phrase." I knew what she meant. How often have I come upon a phrase, a sentence, a sentiment that stood out. As if speaking to me. Capturing what I thought, how I felt, said just the way I would have said it or wished I had. It was not thought before, but once in front of me, I realized it was what I thought. It needed saying. Since found, it stayed with me, to be read and read again, as if by reading it would take root since I may not read this way again. They are joys, these well-turned phrases.

A Well-Turned Phrase

You stood out
in a world of words,
worded just that way,
the way I think and feel
or more,
new thoughts to treasure,
lifting me from ordinary,
such a delicate touch upon a yearning soul.

Were you speaking to me?
Surely so,
else how could you have caught
my eye and ear?
How could you know so much
about me?

I read you and read you again,

savoring a truth found or shared,
wondering what led you to this
and what led me.
And then,
armed with no answers
but comforted still,
I set out again upon this
world of words,
in wait for the next well-turned phrase,
not knowing when or where it will be,
only that it will welcome and shelter me.

—April 1999

37.

"Will you write me a poem about my home room?" I was asked by a new first grade teacher, a friend of my son, Joe. I agreed and spoke with her to get a sense of what was special about this first year and her class and what feelings she wanted to express. My hope was to find the essence of what she wanted to say and express it in a way that reflected it. This is what I wrote. She said it did.

First Home Room

You were my first,
my only,
first home room.
How far we've come together
you and I!
As much as I taught you,
you taught me
as I learned with you.
I saw wonder in your eyes
and it made me wonder.
I heard laughter in your voices
and it made me smile.
I felt your awe at everything new
and I was awed too.

To have touched your lives
touched me,
and as I send you on your way,
my hope, my dream
is that as you reach for the stars—
and you will—
I will be there,

in your minds,
in your hearts,
in your memories of
our home room.

—May 2001

38.

In the movie *The Horse Whisperer*, Robert Redford, the "horse whisperer" on a ranch in Montana, healed horses that had suffered physical abuse and whose spirits were broken. He helped bring them back to allowing a touch and trusting again. Kristen Scott-Thomas was a professional from the city who brought her daughter, Scarlett Johanssen, and her damaged horse to Redford's ranch. As chemistry grew between Redford and Scott-Thomas, he revealed that he had been an architect in Chicago and had left that life for the rustic one he now pursued. She was surprised. He had been married before. Her surprise grew. She asked when he knew it was over. He said, "Knowing is the easy part; saying it out loud is the hard part." How much do we dare not say out loud? And why? To spare someone pain? Ourselves guilt? Fear of unknown consequences? Are favors really done if the truth is unspoken? It reduces the world—theirs and ours—to an illusion. It is not real. The truth cannot be forever kept at bay. It will come out, leaving lost years of deception with no chance to have the time back.

Out Loud

How much knowing goes on inside,
as if unspoken only there resides,
as if unsaid it is not real,
and unfaced we will not feel,
as if kept silent
we could heal.

But thoughts unsaid
are not thoughts undone,
for once thought, their time will come.
The thought comes first;

the words but follow,
fraught with meaning
or numbing hollow,
finally forced on those to tell
or left unsaid a private hell.
Once said the deed is done,
harbored fears now free to run,
opening more than silence
could hide.
Better or worse,
who's to decide?

How much knowing goes on inside,
the knowing the saying cannot abide,
for when all is done and said,
the knowing is easy.
It's the saying we dread.

—April 2004

39.

When do endings begin? Is it when something is finally said or when the unsaying goes on so long it is the same? How long has the ending waited to be proclaimed? There is no fixed point, no same time for anyone. Perhaps it is when the weight becomes too much from living too long with or going too long without.

Endings

When did the ending begin?
Was it the first time we did not
reach back,
or did not reach at all?
When we heard less because
not listening,
or questions not asked because
we did not care?
When we ceased to look
into each other's eyes
and kept our hearts to ourselves—
or worse, did not?
Was it my first look away
or yours?
When did it end?
When did I know?
When did you?

Perhaps we can never say.
No moment yields itself so easily;
the question asked only once done,
no way to know if before
would have been too soon,

if now could have been before,
enough ahead in a possible world
that in time we no longer ask,
but may wonder still.

—April 2004

40.

"I want you to know I believe in your song," Dobie Gray sang in his classic tune "Drift Away," a paean to music that so deeply touches something in us that we are drawn to it and become lost in it. We each have a song, the essence of us, how we live, what we have to say. Don't we all wish for a person so keenly moved by us they would say, "I believe in your song"? I believe in you. I am drawn into the depth of you. They treasure in us what we hold most dear about ourselves. That is our song. Do we sing it? Or is the silence of our unsung melody deafening? We should guard our song jealously and live it passionately.

My Song

I sing to you,
Life,
from my heart,
from my soul,
from the deepest part of me,
shared in our moments alone.
I sing of dreams and longings,
my place in you,
and I soar!

Who is this that draws near
pleased to hear me,
their wait over,
rare spirits hearing their song in mine?
I am them.
They must know more.
They must know me.

To have touched them
is everything,
their finding in me something to believe
in a world that sings of nothing;
it has other concerns.

They are hard to find,
these drifting souls,
with their songs yearning to be heard
along with mine.

—May 2004

41.

In the quirky movie *Joe Versus the Volcano*, Tom Hanks and Meg Ryan took first steps toward a relationship. He said to her, "Who am I? That's the real question, isn't it? Who-who am I? Who are you! What other questions are there?" This goes to the heart of two people reaching for each other. The search for the answer is the journey of our lives. With all we keep inside, our best hope is to find answer enough to take a chance on each other.

Any Other Question

Who am I? Who are you?
Is there any other question?
I'm glad you asked.

We reach for one another
with such hope,
careful at first,
testing until we are sure
or more secure,
but never are, or not for long,
life interrupting,
time rearranging.
Is there forever?

Who am I?
How can I tell you if I do not know?
Still learning myself,
I am more than what you see,
more than what I do.
How much do I show you?
How much can you bear?

How can I tell you what I need from you
if my worry is what you need from me
to keep you here?
Oh,
the burden of holding your interest!

Who are you?
How can I know if you will not tell me?
I look for clues,
observe your cues,
make my guesses,
but will it fall on the ears
of someone not there?
How close do I come to you?
Do you feel me near
or observe me from afar?

I struggle to know you
as I struggle to know me.
Will you be here tomorrow?
Will I?
I must believe we will,
and our time together:
Was I me?
Were you you?

—July 2014

42.

In the movie *Learning to Drive,* Ben Kingsley, a Sikh taxi driver who had been a university professor, was asked by his passenger, Patricia Clarkson, why he teaches driving. He answered, "For a better job, I would have to take off my turban, shave my beard. People think I look dangerous. But this is how I know who I am. And here it is too easy to forget." We might ask ourselves the same. How do we know who we are? What frames of reference do we require? Positions at work? Our place in the family? Being needed? How we are seen? Where we fit? Is it all these things? And when they change or are lost, where does this leave us? Do we know who we are we without them?

Who We Are

When did we first feel ourselves
as separate?
When did first thoughts emerge
not spoken or shown to us?
Who is this
newly arrived on our scene?
When did we first sense
the newcomer was us?

Eyes, arms, voices reach out
telling us who we are,
who will have us,
what they want of us.
We fit here.
Do we know ourselves only
from what they give
and the comfort of place?
Or do we give the fit

only what we must
so they will know us,
so they will keep us?
And if they are gone,
all of them,
what remains with the fit removed?
Where will we belong?
Must there be someone to reassure?

No need to ask as long as the fit
is right,
but as it goes,
do we?
No bearings last forever.
Unmoored,
where do we begin?

Something leads us beyond stopped
or wandering.
There is not but one place for us,
not one fit.
We are not lost,
are more than what is gone,
have much to offer what comes next;
there is still want for it,
want and need for who we are,
always a fit for us ahead.

—May 2015

43.

"Ain't no words for 'I' or 'me' in our language. Just 'us.'" Wise words passed on by the Native American father to his son in the TV movie *Dreamkeeper*. What an uplifting thought! What a sense of belonging! What selflessness! We should all aspire to so much. But it is hard these days. This truth seems to find little favor. Still, we should be aware it is there and within reach.

We and Us

How often I and Me
fail us,
seeming to satisfy for a time,
for the moment,
but always seeking more,
nothing is enough,
the reward short-lived,
unable to keep the emptiness away.

We long for We and Us,
often without knowing.
Others wait too,
wait for us,
not aware the lack they feel
is theirs,
filled only by the touch of another,
only by a walk together,
only by a tenderness and caring
we cannot give ourselves,
just as we wait for them,

not knowing how we needed them
until they are here.

We are more than just ourselves,
or we are lost.

—July 2014

44.

In the movie *Dinner with Friends*, as Andie McDowell and Dennis Quaid heard that the marriage of their close friends was ending, they looked at their own and realized how they too had drifted apart. There was no major confrontation, no precipitating event. There had simply been a slow distancing over the years, with neither knowing when the other left. Quaid described how they had changed over time and his belief that this shifting was inevitable. There was no argument from McDowell, just the forlorn query, "Don't you ever miss me, Gabe?" This question hangs over every parting. The shared histories and memories remain and the recognition it was not nothing.

Do You Miss Me?

Do you ever miss me?
asks the stranger across from me now,
the newcomer the years deliver daily.
Are you wistful for who we once were,
remembering our beginning,
sad at our becoming,
a simpler time when we could not know
the good times would not be enough,
the bad we could not survive?

Do I miss you as we were then?
How could I not?
The memories did not leave with you.
And what of me?
Do you miss me?

But we are left with now.
We could not pick and choose,

too much lost to time,
taken by happenings we could not
or would not stop,
the joy of then with it,
only the ending sadness remains.
Are we better for the time filled with us?
I must believe we are.

—December 2004

45.

In the London stage production *Only The Lonely: The Roy Orbison Story*, Roy Orbison's son, Wesley, had endured much: his father always on the road with no time for him, the death of his mother, the death of his two brothers in a fire that he and Roy's parents survived, his father's remarriage and start of a new family for whom he now had time, and his being left to live with his grandparents. Finally, Roy wanted to reach out to his son. They came together. Roy began to speak. Wesley, still torn with conflicting emotions, went into the kitchen to get a Coke. When he came back, Roy had died of a heart attack. He was devastated, tormented that his father finally had time for him, and he stopped the words of apology. He anguished over this lost chance, mumbling aloud that he had so much he wanted to say. And then the unseen narrator through the mist-filled stage told him to tell his dad now; he could still hear him. His first words were, "Was there something wrong with me, Dad?" I have never heard anything so heartbreaking. To think a child would ask such a question, would ever have this doubt.

Was There Something Wrong With Me?

There are some cuts to the soul
that do not heal,
even if not intended,
even if a worst imagining,
the wound is just as deep,
no less real.
Was it about us?
It is how it feels,
even if our minds know better,
and others tell us it is not so,

we cannot help but wonder.

We are weighed down
with words said or never spoken,
with time never there for us,
with actions withheld while
we waited.
We did not matter or so it feels,
always hoping—for what?
To go back?
Another chance?
More time?

Can enough ever be said,
ever be done
to repair?
We can come close,
can do all we can,
but cannot undo,
cannot erase,
remnants always remain.

But repair we must,
or try.
There is always time.
Whatever time is left,
there is time.
With a dying breath,
there is time.
Only time can say too late.
Even then, from the grave
we must believe it is said,
and we mattered all along.

Tell someone—
a child, a person at every age—
all that is right with them,
everyone needing to hear it,
no one hearing it enough.

—March 2019

46.

"There's no one else in your world, is there?" Though said to me in jest, there is always some truth, otherwise there would be nothing to jest about. It is no different for anyone. We each view the world through isolated eyes and see only what we see. No one else perceives the same. We occupy a cloistered space. Others come as close as they can, understand us the best they are able or as much as we allow. The rest of us is inside looking out, seeing the closeness of others, approaching as near to them as we can and grateful for them.

My World

There is no one else in my world,
you say,
in jest I know,
but clearly something prompts you.
The same is no less for you,
your world as solitary as mine,
seen only by you;
no one has your eyes.
You, like me, see others near,
but close is not here.

We allow others in,
not too far, not too long;
areas are still reserved just for us,
well hidden,
though sending signs they are there.
It keeps you coming back to me,
and me to you.

So be not so quick to judge me;
there is a plank in your eye.
We draw lines differently around
our circled worlds,
but close enough to want more.
I will let you further
into my world
if you let me into yours.
You go first.

—June 2004

47.

At a legal conference I attended, one of the speakers spoke with assuredness on the topic at hand. I commended her eloquence. She confessed she did not know as much as it seemed. "Life is a bluff," she said. "How do you think I go through life?" Are we much the same, putting on airs of confidence to mask knowing less? Why do it? Perhaps because we can and will continue so long as the bluff is not called.

Life Is a Bluff

Put your best foot forward,
your best face on,
as we are told and trained to do,
hoping it will be enough
to survive the moment,
knowing we are not as good as that.
Others do it too
in this high-stakes game.
Most times it is enough if
no one delves too deeply;
they are bluffing too,
everyone seeming better
or more secure
than they are.

No problem,
so long as they are as good
as they need to be,
as the bluff goes on,
and the game continues.
Does the bluff never end?

Could we tell?
Do we care?
Is life ever more than a bluff
by someone?

—July 2015

48.

At another legal conference, one presentation was particularly impressive. I complimented the speaker, who candidly said, "If only these people knew what I was really thinking." This is a familiar disconnect. How often have we mouthed words in conversation, enough to get by, with our minds somewhere else? Where do we go? The places are endless, sometimes anywhere but here, or we may just roam, the conversation not enough to hold our interest or require our undivided attention.

If They Only Knew

Eyes upon me,
the audience rapt,
hanging on my every word,
upon the wisdom they hear,
impressed with my devotion to the cause,
a promise made to them,
then the applause.
The god of approval is satisfied.

Behind the sage advice,
the learned instruction,
the parroted words,
my mind has taken flight,
searching for more meaning
or better drawn.

I have been where they are
and back.
I am here,
passing on what is asked,

lost in thoughts of elsewhere,
anywhere.
If they only knew
for all I say,
I am not really here.

—March 2016

49.

Are we as talented as others think or just more capable than them? If successful, we are seen that way. We play the role as we exude confidence and lack of worry or concern. The image grows, sometimes exceeding our limits. We embrace this or at least do not disavow it, relishing the praise whether deserved or not. Why turn it down? We'll take what is handed to us. Deep down, we know it is not as true as others would believe. The image is stalked by the fear of being found out. One question away from being exposed. What if we cannot live up? The wait goes on for the illusion to end until, in time, it no longer matters.

Found Out

Another day survived as who
we seem to be,
so knowledgeable,
so much well done.
No one suspects or looks too close
at who struggles beneath to stay afloat,
one question away from
what we do not know.
We do enough to stave off the asking,
letting you believe what you will.
Why tell you differently?

It starts with who we are expected to be
or with the first success,
no going back;
it must be preserved at all cost,
the pretending never too much,
the barter of our selves.

How wearing the wait to be found out
when we know better.

Do we excel so much?
Or do others,
daunted by our seeming ease,
think themselves less,
unaware doubt plagues us all,
just hidden better by some?
We are no different.
Do we owe them anything?

And so we go another day
living up to the exalted us,
imposter or not,
wondering:
Will this be the day
we are found out?

—December 2007

50.

In the movie *Love and Other Drugs,* Jake Gyllenhaal, a drug representative, became involved with Anne Hathaway who suffered from Parkinson's. He broke up with her, unsure whether he could handle her illness. Distraught at being without her, he pleaded to get back together. She resisted, not wanting to be a burden to him as her condition worsened. He told her that he needed her. She said she would need him more. He tried to assure her he would be there. She countered that she could not ask him to do that. He said, "You didn't." Then he told her, "I have never known anyone who actually believed that I was enough. Until I met you. And then you made me believe it, too. So, uh … unfortunately … I need you. And you need me." Isn't this what we all want—to be able to believe we are enough for someone we love?

Am I Enough?

Am I enough for you to stay?
This is my fear.
Is it yours?

I try to please,
work to entertain,
anything to hold your interest,
alert for any sign of your tiring,
your searching elsewhere.
What more must I do?
as the dance goes on,
exhausting,
the pressure of more.
Will I ever be enough?
and the pain of having to wonder,

the dread of having to ask.
Are we doomed if I
must always do something
to hold you?

We cannot be forced,
cannot live in a world of more,
a world of never enough,
cannot forever mask what we do not have,
pretense, trying only go so far.
We cannot survive efforts
without end
that allow no break,
no time when,
not having to try,
we are enough for each other.

And so I must ask,
Am I enough for you?
Are you enough for me?

—February 2012

51.

In an episode of the TV series *Ally McBeal,* Ally, with no romantic involvement at the moment, wondered whether she should settle for someone just to not be alone. Her friend Renee disagreed and said, "There's nothing lonelier that being with the wrong guy." Renee was right. With the wrong person, there is nothing to share. Too much held back. Too much doing without. Too much pretense. No trust. No comfort. No way to live.

The Loneliest Place

I am lonely,
not for you—
you are here—
much more,
I am lonely for me,
for my missing self when I am with you,
what I will not share,
kept behind the face,
appearances must be maintained,
but huddled in loneliness,
crying out in muted pain.

Others surround me;
we talk,
act our social ways,
but nothing coaxes me from my self.
I do not trust,
feel on my own,
give only enough to outlast the moment,
waiting for someone
who senses something missing,

who knows there is more,
someone to look,
someone to care,
someone who can see
what is obvious to me,
not knowing who I wait for,
knowing only they have not come
and are not you.

—May 1999

52.

In the Loving Spoonful's hit recording "Darling Be Home Soon," the urging to be home soon is "for the great relief of having you to talk to." Don't we all wish for this in a relationship: to have such connection with another that we feel great relief at having them to talk to? They are special. They get us. They feel us. No one else will do.

The Great Relief

You are on your way.
For what do I wait?
For what do I want?
More than your being here,
presence is easy.
More than what you have done or can do,
impressed as I may be.
You have overwhelmed my defenses,
scaled my walls,
found me,
convinced me
not to limit what I say,
guard what I feel,
you will care for me,
and there is such easing when
I do,
newly felt,
as I eagerly await your return
and the great relief of having you
to talk to.

—February 2019

53.

In the play and movie *Shirley Valentine*, Shirley, tired and worn of life, longed to get away to Greece on holiday. Her husband dismissed this as foolishness. Shirley lamented, "I have allowed myself to lead this little life, when inside me there was so much more. And it's all gone unused. And now it never will be. Why do we get all this life if we don't ever use it?" She went to Greece alone. What stores of unused life have we? It changes as more of life is spent and picks up speed as time runs out. Not a bucket list. More fundamental. It dips into our psyche where reside things kept inside, put off, given up, as our lives are shrunk to what time and circumstance have allowed. We know it is there from feelings of emptiness and longing. We should live as much of unused life as we are able, not mourn its passing before its time.

Unused Life

The walls close in,
the door shutting,
a premature burial advancing
on my unused life.
Hopes, dreams not given up for dead,
though put off so long there is
no difference,
make their presence known.
They are alive!
The lives unlived,
the selves not yet become,
still within sight,
believed within reach,
their absence felt

as if I am meant to be somewhere else,
even as the future and the end
take them further from me.
What a store of unused life I have!

Their voices call out,
letting me know they are near,
pleading not to be forgotten,
waiting patiently,
their language melancholy and longing
that I have not come for them,
as they find me in places I go to dream
and touch me harder.

Is this the day when I reach back?
Or plod along as if they are not there,
only dreams not meant to stay,
temporary respite before returning me
to a world without them?

Each time I venture near
does part of me stay
until I am hollow,
my unused life given up on me?
No!
I am not over yet!
Unused life,
I am coming!

—November 2014

54.

In Frank Sinatra's iconic song "My Way," most focus on the line "I did it my way." This is the appeal of the song, isn't it? I am struck by the words just before that: "To think I did all that." We have each done "all that" by the sheer act of living. The panorama of our lives is vast. What we faced. How we coped. The prices we paid. The memories we built. It may not be heroic deeds or have the maverick approach of "my way." It may include desperate times, tragedy and comedy. It is everything that brought us here. We should appreciate what we have done. We have survived. We are still standing. Yes, we—you and I—have done "all that."

Done All That

My life can seem detached
when I look back,
surreal,
like observing someone else,
another's life lived,
my being there only dimly recalled.

It did not seem so much at the time,
perhaps was not,
but life lived adds up:
what I have said,
what I have done,
people come and gone,
happenings and close calls,
the undone, the never was,
all spread before me.

How did I do all that?
Past runs into past,
decades into years,
when giving way to done
or no more time,
even with details blurring,
memory not keeping up.
To think this was me!

Getting here took much,
not to be waved off as too little,
the sum of me.
I was there,
I am here,
I left a mark.
I did all that.

—March 2010

55.

In the movie *Tombstone,* Doc Holliday (Val Kilmer), on his sickbed in the sanitarium, asked Wyatt Earp (Kurt Russell) what he wanted out of life. Wyatt said he just wanted to live a normal life. Doc said, "There's no normal life Wyatt. It's just life. Get on with it." Doc was right. Life is complex. Circumstances change. People are unique. My life is not yours. Perhaps the closest we can come to normal is to recognize common values and to live with some degree of predictability. We cannot prepare for everything. There must be some ground that does not shift. What is normal? Only we can say for us, and it changes with age and time.

A Normal Life

We hear of a normal life,
are told it is there for the taking,
unnamed others have it,
and we falling short because
we do not know what it is,
this mythic wonderland,
its seeming presence everywhere but us,
an illusion of our making,
a happiness of others eluding us.

They do not share failings
we can see,
have outward perfection
we know is not real,
yet we cling to the notion of better elsewhere,
we, the outlier,
not allowing for demons everywhere
or the normal others see in us.

This vision of others and better,
always on sale,
is a figment.
There is no measuring up to what
is not there,
only a fantasy to keep the pursuit alive;
we must have it,
our blame if we have somehow missed
in ways we do not know.
Where is it?
How do I get there?

Why this envy for someone else's life?
We cannot see their cost,
all are adrift on the same sea,
no one has made it to shore.
No normal,
just life,
with demands upon us all,
our responses our own,
our best the normal for us.

—November 2006

56.

At a Continuing Legal Education seminar, a presentation was made to honor a retiring family law judge. In accepting the award, she spoke of all she had witnessed in her many years on the bench—the heartaches, the heartbreaks, the family violence, people treated in ways she would never have imagined. As she prepared to take her leave, she commented, "I'm thankful for my humdrum life." On its face, such a life may have little appeal. There is a negative connotation. We struggle to avoid being relegated to ordinary. We want the most of what life has to offer, to be in the middle of the fray, not passed by. We worry too about how we will be seen by others. What peak experiences set us apart? Will we be written off as not interesting? Nothing special? Not worth the time? And so comes the temptation to embellish. Things are described in glowing terms as more than they were or are. My experience tops yours or I had one like it. The media feeds the need. Advertising promotes it. The pace is frenetic. To what extent do we go along, not really wanting the ride but afraid to say no?

A Humdrum Life

I have always shunned a humdrum life
as if it were a sitting out,
a walking away,
a viewing from afar,
the quickened pace proof I am alive,
leaving nothing behind,
not left out.

The game goes on as lesser souls vie.
How can I let them win if I am
not made less,

even if I have no interest,
even if there is no prize,
just no loss,
and the weariness of living
someone else's world?

There is comfort in knowing
humdrum moments are there,
where calm resides,
a breath is taken,
extremes relax,
so much missed
not mattering so much,
past disdain fades.

There is much to value here,
waiting while I chased after wind,
not ready before now,
welcoming my approach,
always with time for me.

—November 2014

IV. INWARD LOOKS

57.

There is great pressure to fit in. We have a need to belong. The longer we are at it, we may find ourselves moving away from who we are and want to be. We become what situations call for, a fluid us. It is no worry up to a point. But where is the line? Our put-aside self does not sit quietly. It wants back in. We can feel the pull, the discomfort, even as we resist, until fitting in is no longer worth the cost if we have that luxury.

Trying So Hard

Faces strained,
sometimes laughter,
other times pasted smiles,
how can they hold it so long?
Chattering away,
pretending whatever needs to be true
for now,
as so the conversation goes.

Such animation! So intense!
Trying so hard in chase after what?
To belong? To please?
Acceptance? Approval?

To not be left behind
as the world and others go on?

What if they stop?
Faces relax into what they feel,
happy or sad,
shades in between,
the fever broken.
We cannot be fluid forever.

What is left? What is true?
Then the smiles are back,
hastened before the answer.
It is sometimes easier to try this hard
than to ask.

—October 1999

58.

We are careful what we show to others, disclosing more to some but never all. There is an unsaid world of things kept inside. The fears are many: shame, embarrassment, being judged, not hurting others, not being understood, not appreciated, rejected, or perhaps simply to match our outer face, each the price of saying too much. Deeper parts of our selves are withheld to live on if all else fails. This is a dangerous game we play, this holding back. We risk finding too late that we held back too much. Our unrevealed selves have never been known, never entered the world where we moved under the guise of a partial self. How tragic! It is a lonely place, this unsaid world.

The Unsaid World

There is a place within
where gather unspoken thoughts
we dare not share,
not willing to trust
because we cannot be sure,
where can be said
what we would never say,
conversing with ourselves,
where fears reside and
discontent simmers and
decisions are left in limbo,
harbored without a sound
lest we give them too much life,
too much of us.

Once said, it is released,
no longer within our reach,
now alive for more than us,

and we never seen the same again,
in its wake what kept them silent
when, unsaid, it was there all along,
not needing saying to be real,
shadowing us either way,
leaving us to add
to a new unsaid world
what we have learned.

It is lonely in this unspoken world,
a recluse
waiting until safe to speak,
a day that never comes,
never giving anyone a chance to live up,
they may be more welcoming than we know,
we, hardest upon ourselves.

Will no one come for me?
Does no one know I am here?

—July 2014

59.

We all close off, some more than others. When did we first hold back? Was it when we learned the safest gesture can have conditions, acceptance and approval can always be at risk? Do we make assumptions of doubt and stand back, finding greater certainty there than in being wrong? Why is the unknown so threatening? Yes, there is risk, but openness offers more—with all the chance of failing, with the peril of being hurt. However bruised, we will survive. This is life. Not in hiding, but in daring.

Closed Off

When did the closing off begin?
this keeping of others at a distance,
even the best,
too far away to see my distress,
knowing they would help if they knew,
but even this not enough,
sacrificing their touch to demands of forever,
doubting it will last,
not knowing how they will greet parts of me
met for the first time.

Will they judge?
Will they leave?
What risk!
If I am wrong, it is too late,
even the little closing off has to give
is better than nothing.
So unfair to them.
So unfair to me.

Give them a chance!
I know, I know.
It is easy to say,
but fear gives no quarter,
it need do nothing,
we do it all.
And so they wait at the gate to help
until, worn from the waiting,
they walk away,
and I close off more,
knowing I was right.

—October 2014

60.

We face a demanding world. Compromises, trade-offs, pragmatic sufferances are required. What does this take from us? We are still here, but is there less of us? When does our going become gone? We may be vaguely conscious of our leaving but rarely of how far we have moved. Will we look about one day and find we are nowhere to be found? Only we can call a halt. Put some limits. Recall the beginning, everything ahead. Return to the dreams, even if by a different way. Reformulate them if we must. We are not gone. There is still much to be done.

Going, Going ... Gone?

There is a war afoot for our attention
and much more,
for our soul and self,
with distractions and demands,
anything to divert from you and me,
and so the self is put aside,
on hold,
given up in pieces,
filling just the moment,
each stolen from those left,
while we tend to the inane
and mundane,
something for everyone—
whose hand is out today?
It adds up.

I could feel it as it happened,
slow as it seemed,
and temporary,

can see myself going more clearly now.
Is it too late?

No!
Not all gone! Not yet!
Enough left to pull me back,
still time for lines to be drawn,
for slow turns and about-faces.
No forks in this road back;
I know the way,
while my put-aside self
waits hopefully for my return.

—May 1999

61.

How much do we become who others want us to be? It depends. The considerations are many: who they are; is it family duty or business obligation; is it fair; is it reasonable; what leeway do we have to resist; will we say no even if we can? Our responses bridge this spectrum. We are different things to different people.

Chameleon

Who am I?
you ask.
Who do you want me to be?
I can change colors
to match your portrait of me,
satisfying commissions for my time
and my craving for them,
and I can change back,
turn on a dime.
I know how to work the room.
Where am I in this kaleidoscope?
Where is the fixed point for the turning
and return,
or does this move too?

As the colors fade and leave
with the slowing of the asks,
as we approach black,
do we wish the colors back?

Or do we find
in the last to go
the generous, driven soul before
the changing of the colors began?

—April 2019

62.

We have images of ourselves as we think others see us, as we want to be seen, as we see ourselves. Some carry this further and refer to this image of themselves in the third person. When I hear this, I am tempted to say, "Isn't that you? Why not just talk about you?" We all play to these images and the personae they create. We work to stay in character. The danger is the image taking over. Giving it our name personifies it, accords a separate presence we may feel must be lived up to. Fealty is to what we have named. But the self must not become the servant of the image. We must hold the reins. No image will stay forever.

The Third Person

I am shadowed by a stranger
passing as me,
familiar to those who know me.
He tries to please them;
they ask much of him
and are clear as to what they want.
He does much of what I do,
less of what I want to do,
not always as I would do it.

They seem to like him,
though how much
I cannot tell,
but it is better than without him.
I will keep him close to me,
let him do as he must
to satisfy
and keep them here.

What should I call him?
Others call him me.
Perhaps I will too,
so they will know.

—July 2014

63.

However we see ourselves, no matter how much we try to be seen that way, we must wonder: what do others see? How closely do our efforts match how we are looked upon? How much do we not know? What private judgments, what untold reservations are kept from us? We may never know. But known or not, this looked-upon world is there.

The Looked-Upon World

We are looked upon
in every line of vision,
random or played to,
and we know it,
even dress for it—
how we think we are viewed
or want to be.

What do they see?
Not ours to judge.
We can only control so much,
so often never told the verdict,
never hear the whispers,
never notice the sidelong glances,
the knowing looks,
never see behind the curtain
of this looked-upon world.
How far short are we there?
They cover well.
Is face value what it seems?

What if we knew?
Would we alter the image

or remain nestled in its palm,
pretending not to know
lest we must do something,
safer there,
not at the whim or the pleasing of
someone not us,
someone not even our image?

—June 2019

64.

Emotions descend as the offspring of other happenings. They cannot be summoned or forced. We cannot decide to feel a certain way. They arise from what we have done or failed to do, from apprehension about what is to come, from things that have happened. We cannot order them away. They will leave only when spent. Even then, signs they were there remain. It is hard sometimes to describe what we feel. But there is a reason we feel as we do. Named or not, they will hold us until what brought them to us ends. We cannot help the way we feel. We can always control what we do. The choices are ours no matter how conflicted we may be.

Emotions

What do I feel?
I can scarcely say.
The feelings come at me
from all sides,
and from nowhere I can tell,
battling for dominance,
sometimes a struggle to survive,
much less explain,
there is no time,
the effort is too much,
my attention diverted
to other things.

I ride the wave
or am swept with it,
holding on,
I will look inside later,
for now only this.

At times I reach to understand,
hesitant to look too closely,
soon turned away by something new,
more pressing,
or the retreat of not wanting to know.

Can I return to the safety
before their coming?
Was it ever safe?
Was there no way to hold them off?

What do I feel?
I can scarcely say.
I can only feel as I do.

—November 2012

65.

Much pain goes unexpressed, especially for men. It is thought by some to be a sign of weakness. The macho image must be kept up. Once lost, it is gone for good. But not flinching has a price. Unexpressed is not unfelt. The Stoic still hurts. And men suffer for it.

Unspoken Pain

Tears do not come easily for men,
and so women cry alone,
and men suffer without sound,
unshed, unshared emotion.
They dare not tell,
if they cannot resist
they are no different,
they are gone.

Who is this that stares back
through the gathering tear?
Who am I now?
Who will want me?

It is too much,
and so we dry our eyes and our hearts,
and hold tight,
slowed with unspoken pain,
as we stumble on
in unbroken flight.

—May 1998

66.

We burden ourselves and each other with demands that go too far and needs that cannot be met. When the falling short occurs, we can feel a sense of failure, disappointment turned our way, the resentment of unfairness, defenses marshaled. Left unattended, the burdens grow and turn to distance. Someone must go first if we are not to lose one another. We are better with the burdens eased. Life becomes more lenient and more real. We can see more than a load shouldered and carried or not. We can see the person under the weight giving their best.

The Burdens

Oh,
the burdens we put on one another
and ourselves,
with expectations fanciful or not
and demands fair or not
and what we withhold to get
our way.
No one is enough all the time.

So comes defending
and striking back with criticism
and complaint,
and retreat to corners further away,
in the name of missing trust
and needed shield,
as so the downward spiral goes
until the first reach out before
it is too late,
in the hope of a reach back,

and I see you and you see me
as we were before the conflict began.

Let me have for that moment
the sweet vision of who we were
before the burdens,
before we found ourselves
at the mercy of what
we could not or would not stop.

—January 2007

67.

Grudges outlive their beginning and early rancor. They are mired in the past, fixated on wrongs long over, allowing no effort to go beyond, offering no future. Memory is their hold, not letting go their staying power. Life moving on is their weakness and better things to do their ending. Which it will be is our choice.

The Grudge

The grudge
has come for me again,
playing upon my anger,
assuring me in my righteousness,
no concern for what it is taking,
bleeding my time from better spent,
restraining me in the past,
a mindless holding on,
forget the reason why.

It requires little from us,
needs no tending,
just that we remain in place,
fearing only peace of mind's approach,
it cannot offer that
as combat for us is waged.

The grudge,
known and comfortable in its way,
it is easier to stay,
but it cannot outlast the promise
of tomorrow,
moving on the only way there,

as the tightness inside subsides,
fists unclench,
hatred now forgotten or pointless,
fresh air inhaled,
new energy rising,
and rest,
missing so long,
finally here.

—November 2006

68.

Silence. It can be hard to find. Noise everywhere. The din can seem unending. Focus can be hard to maintain. Reflection and insight must fight for a place. Sometimes what we need is our aloneness in silence. Let our minds stop racing. Most things can wait. Private moments can be spared. The pace will quicken soon enough. We need this time to clear and slow our thinking. Renewed, we will be better.

Silence

Noise, clamor,
background volumes—
they compete for our attention
like a willful child,
overpowering other senses,
laying hold of now
and claims to our looking ahead.
If it can keep us for an instant,
it postpones our going,
forcing us to endure its mindless ramblings,
silence our only shelter
if we will make the time.

Listen
to the beauty of the silence,
voices quieted,
sounds muffled,
still much to hear but wordless.
Thoughts no longer crowded out,
inner speakings emerge;
my mind freed
turns to remembrances and imaginings ahead,

new conquests,
insights waiting to be heard,
the slowing of my latest struggles,
aspects of self of no interest to others,
all needing just quieted moments
to make their case.

I will stay for a while,
not linger too long,
too much calls me back,
I will be there soon enough.
Refreshed,
I will make time for more.

—February 1999

69.

The loss of feeling special can be among the hardest to endure. It is appreciated most when no longer there, not experienced before then as gone. Even then it is possessive to the end, taking root in memories of what once was.

Special

Special,
what brings you to me?
What keeps you here?
bursting as you did to surprise me,
too soon taken for granted,
so sure you were forever.

Are you moment to moment
as much as we,
deciding when you will come,
when you will go?
Do I have no say?
Am I always at risk of someone else?

When you are no more,
did you go or were you never here?
this the cruelest thought—
what never was.
Is the illusion less when
it was enough at the time?
Can the feeling so real
be undone if not here now?

They each have their place,
even if there remains only
the crestfallen lament:
I thought I was special,
and the hope that though
I no longer am
does not mean I never was.

Special,
will I feel you again?

—May 2019

70.

A good friend lost his mother. She was not young and had a full life. It was not unexpected. She was not in good health. But the loss struck no less deep. As my friend said, "This was my mother." Gone was the unconditional love, the unqualified acceptance, the refuge. No judgment. We all need that and feel it deeply when it is gone.

One Less Safe Place

Where am I to turn now
with barbarians at the gate?
My defenses have limits;
even I need rest—
somewhere to not try so hard,
somewhere that will have me
even if I am not strong,
even if I fail,
where I can regroup.

There are few like this,
mothers first,
and I forever her child,
and she is gone.

Let the world judge me as it will;
let others have me or not.
I am always welcome here,
always home,
until there is no more,
no more mothering ahead,

no more caring words to be said,
leaving me more on my own
as I turn to face
a world with one less safe place.

—December 2013

71.

There it is again: the bump in the night, out of the darkness. What could it be? My mind races as I struggle to define it, matching it to what I know, working to explain it away, tie it to something benign, anything to avoid another search that will end like all the rest— nothing there or nothing new, always able to be explained, this time no different, the sound was the same. Or was it? Was there the slightest change? Let me run through the list again of what it could be. Have I missed something?

The Bump in the Night

What was that sound?
Did you hear it?
Why did it wake me?
Could it be nothing?
Was it a dream?
Did I hear it at all?
Did someone get in?

But how?
The alarm did not go off.
No sound of glass breaking,
no window or door being forced.
no sound like the weight of a foot.
Could it be the house creaking,
beams settling or shifting,
the ground subsiding
and the house with it?

Could something have fallen?
An object? a fixture?

Not an appliance;
there was no metallic ring,
nothing is running.

Perhaps it was nothing,
just the sound of the house getting older.
No point in getting up;
I have been there before.
It is always the same: no one there.
Is it different this time,
the smallest change that should
signal alarm,
as I lie here in wait
until they emerge from the darkness
or retreat into mornings light?

Wait! There it is again.
This changes everything.
Was it the same?
Is it louder? Is it closer?
Am I listening too hard?
Was I asleep?
No, I heard it. I'm sure.
Is it back? Is someone there?
Should I go check?

—May 2010

72.

My Aunt Pat died on Thursday, May 29, 2014. It was not sudden. She lived a full life. We were surprised she held on so long. The accolades of a life well-lived poured in. They were well-deserved. It was a special loss for me. She was the last of my mother's siblings. My parents, grandparents—all gone. She was the last link with my grandmother's house in New Orleans. I wrote of what this meant to me in "The House" in my book *Defining Moments*. Aunt Pat was there to the end. I am alone with the memories now. I miss her deeply. I wish you could have known her.

Aunt Pat Gone

There never was a time for me
when there was no Aunt Pat
and now there is.
Not sudden,
expected,
merciful.
Her time had come and
I feel it heavily.

Not a piercing pain of loss.
No,
more a growing sense of gone,
a taking of me further from my past,
a leaving of me in a world less familiar,
with fewer knowns,
without the comfort of knowing
she is here.

Aunt Pat,
I thank you for all the times
we had together
—did you gather them with you
as you left—
as time takes on ever more meaning
with your passing?

—May 2014

73.

Do we have a soulmate somewhere? More than one? Some say we do. Beguiled, we search through those we meet unsure of what we seek. No one seems to measure up, the reasons why not mattering, just names given why this is not the one. What is missing? We cannot say, only that we will know when it is found, with life on hold until we do, until life ends and we never did. We deserve better. We should not bind ourselves to a standard no one can meet that will leave us stranded and alone.

Soulmate

Soulmate,
where have you been?
you who knows me best,
sees me without my being there,
senses me without my showing,
welcomes me without asking.

I hear of you from others,
am told you are there.
Why have we never met?
I embrace those who try
but feel nothing or not enough.
How will I know you?

Do I ask too much,
afraid of being left with too little,
settling for without while I wait?
Is there someone better?
Did I look so closely
no one can survive?

And so the wait goes on,
as do those who approach
until
I am left with only me,
never choosing wrong,
never choosing at all,
demanding everything,
left with nothing.

Soulmate,
why did you not show yourself?
Or did you?
Have you come and gone?

—August 2015

74.

It can be unsettling when someone usually upbeat is suddenly down. Voice slowed by sadness. Flat affect. The slump of resignation. If they can be beaten down, what chance do the rest of us have? We realize the hope we get from them. And then they resurrect. Resilience returns. If they can, it is there for us too. Their inspiration remains, and we owe them.

No Hope

Life takes many prisoners,
lays hold of most of us,
but for some it seems less.
Do they fight back more?
Is there less to resist?
Are appearances what they seem?

No matter,
we lean on them just the same,
proof life can be survived and thrive.
There is a point to the struggle,
and hope;
if they made it,
we can too.
Until they falter, even fall,
or give up the fight for a time,
and then they are us,
and we are sorry for them.

If they can be taken,
what have we left to turn to?
Who can make it now?

Has life come for you?
What are the rest of us to do?
Rise again!
Come back for us.

—August 2006

75.

Trust issues. From what depths do they arise? Why so hesitant to take a chance? It goes deep: doubts of self-worth, fears of rejection, lessons learned, not knowing the fate of future gambles. We play it safe, waiting for assurances not to be found, preparing for a distancing we hasten by what we will not give. We should do more. Take risks, even if small at first. We must start somewhere.

Trust Issues

Why do I keep so much from you?
Is it you or me?
I have shown you enough
to bring you here,
must I reveal more for you to stay?
How can I know if you will?
When you leave,
as I have conjured you will,
what is left?

Nothing if I have given all,
so I keep a reserve of more,
ready, waiting.
Will it ever be spent?
Who is worthy?
Must it be held back too?
How much to give,
how much to save,
how much is enough?
Must enough always be the least?

And so I hold on to more of me,
keeping you ever further away,
I never gave you a chance;
I left first.
They are hard,
these trust issues,

—September 2017

V.   RANDOM THOUGHTS

76.

One overcast winter day, the trees had dropped their leaves, exposing bare branches against a gray sky. The contrast was vivid. No in between. Nothing blurred. An interrupting moment of clarity in a hurried world. Then the calm of the moment passed. It was on to next things.

Starkness

Bare branches pierce a canvas sky,
moon in white hangs on a cloudless night,
stars shine beyond urban reach,
sun's first peak of mornings light,
day, night all to itself,
taking time to speak to me.

Starkness,
what is your appeal?
Do you remind all is not a blur,
life is not lost in endless sameness,
merged into roteness.
There can be cleanness to what we do.
Our choices matter;

they could not be anything;
they have their reason.

Do I stand out as well?
not lost in shades of every color
fading into the rest,
ever sizing up who I am
in a world of gray,
until looking back
I cannot make myself out,
I fit in too well,
wondering
how to bring the color back.

—April 1999

77.

Sometimes only gray will do. A break from colliding worlds, all competing, black or white, all or none, win or lose, zero sum. Must we go gray for a while? It can be warming, even welcoming. We will return to black or white soon enough.

Gray

Why, sometimes,
am I content with gray,
in sky, in thought, in how I feel?
No peaks, no valleys,
just retreat from the claims upon
every sense,
conflict without point or end,
so much at odds,
so many on edge.

Oh,
the bleakness of never-ending strife!
Black or white can overwhelm with
insistence not put off,
and we marooned in a sea of others,
all straining at the oar.

Where is respite?
Where to fall back until renewed?
Comfort can be found for a time
in a world of gray,
nothing to decide.

The rest can wait,
at least for now,
no summons to action while resting there
until the call to arms sounds again.

—April 1999

78.

Summer in New Orleans. The heat, the humidity—it does not end. And then, just when hope is lost for summer's close, we step out one morning and there is change. Not much. Not yet. But different in a way that promises more. It is cooler. It will become cooler still. We rejoice, all the while aware how little it takes to lift our thermal despair.

The Summer

> I stepped out,
> braced for the blast of heat,
> readied for the weight of the air,
> heavy and closed all around,
> as I did how many mornings past,
> but it was not there.
>
> Not all gone,
> but enough to know it was missing,
> in its place almost a chill
> that slapped my face,
> morning air crisp and cool,
> or so it seems
> when you are desperate.
>
> What a surprise!
> I was stopped in my tracks,
> basking in the change,
> the long wait finally over,
> the summer that would not end
> has broken.
>
> —October 1998

79.

Autumn's arrival in New Orleans is detected only by those who live there. Described to others, it would still be summer. New Orleanians must be thankful for what they can get.

Autumn Coming

Everywhere
the leaves are changing,
colors turned to flaming
red and gold and orange,
but not here;
they only fade and fall
much as they were.

Temperatures dropping elsewhere,
crisp and cool, a snap in the air,
but not here;
the shuffle goes on,
the wait for winter on its way.

Bundle up,
heating on,
but not here;
there is no cold to come,
only a degree here or there,
the sweat only slowed, never dried,
summer never far.

But we can rejoice
nonetheless,
like all the rest,
and give thanks—
it is autumn in New Orleans.

—October 1998

80.

The Mad Men follow us everywhere. They promise everything. Take this. Buy that. Wear the latest. We will be happy. Take their word for it. Everyone else has one. Do you want to be left out? Not fit in? Stand out as different? Can you not afford it? Don't belong with the in-crowd? And so it goes until the next product launch. Endless novelty. More is better. No matter that we do not need or want. They create that too, unless we learn to resist. Not all at once. We cannot opt out. Be selective. Draw lines. Do something for yourself. Push back against the siren calls.

The Siren Calls

They are all about,
calls enticing us out of ourselves,
seductive, attractive,
packaged it seems for us,
newly spun wants and needs
not designed to stay,
just hold the spot until replaced,
appealing with promises of bliss
or escape,
or no more than more,
and the fear of left out or left behind,
as the sirens prey upon our weakened state
with the newest and the best,
there is no end,
all held out to the waiting crowd
desperate to believe.
I must have it.

Have we learned nothing
from their allure,
how little they have to give?
Not even a pretense it will last,
no future, only now,
unless we begin the turn
to ground ourselves once again,
not just part of the crowd,
back to a life
beyond the bauble
and the babble.

—December 2003

81.

Heroes are not so different from you and me. They were called to act when we were not or before we are. Once gone public, they inspire us. We are capable of more than we think. If forced, perhaps we could do this too. They include more than grand actions and widespread acclaim. Quiet acts of heroism take place every day, unseen, unknown, unappreciated except by a few. You are someone's hero without knowing, inspiring them with what you say and do, how you live, your steady meeting of responsibility, not for praise or accolades, but because something needed doing, someone had to do it, and that someone was you. We are all heroes to someone. We should be aware of this and try to live up to it.

Heroes

Heroes,
where are you when I need you?
How will I find you?
How did you know what to do
before you did?
You inspire others to their reach,
leading into chaos
and returning,
the stars are closer than we think.

We are unaware of our need for you
until you appear,
showing what can be done,
drawing us to the possible,
what could be in us,
allowing us the safety of seeing it
before our turn.

We are heroes more than we know
in ways still to be revealed,
in calls yet to come,
in quiet living not celebrated
but saving in ways we will never know,
under the watchful eye of someone,
already a hero to them.

—January 2018

82.

"Why did this happen to me?" Who has not said this? Who has not thought it? We could as well ask, "Why not?" We have no free pass. We can be angry at what happened. Rage that it is unfair. The randomness of tragedy goes on. Some may seem unscathed. They are not. Unseen hells may be the worst. For all we have suffered, others have too, some much more. How we handle misfortune defines us. Sorrow and loss are personal and lonely, yet we have something to offer each other for what we have gone through—a measure of comfort, a helping hand, no more than our presence if we are at a loss as to what to say. Many times, this is enough.

Misfortune

Misfortunes great and small
befall us all,
but ours come just for us,
none like it
close as they may seem,
each with its own pain
beyond the most earnest embrace,
the wishes well doing what they can.

There is no better,
no worse
in this world of distress.
How can I know the price you pay
or you, mine?
Too much is carried within and silent,
but there does issue from us,
if we will let it,
the thanks we feel for your trying.

For all we must carry alone,
there is much to share,
forced to face what we did,
seeing that you made it too,
bound together
by what we have lived through.

—January 2006

83.

We describe some persons as jaded. The impulse may be to think they do not care. I believe the opposite is true. They care too much. They seek safety in suspicion and retreat, convinced there is so little chance it is not worth the effort. If they do not hope, they will not be disappointed. We should reach out to them. More of what we say is heard than we may think. More is thought over after we are gone. Despair is not final. Nothing stays the same. Changes will come with or without them. They should have a say no matter the odds. These change too.

Jaded

The jaded
may be the most hurt among us,
let down so often
they are afraid to believe,
they care too much,
withdraw too far as trust goes missing,
guarding what dreams they have left
lest they be taken too.
But hope survives even this,
keeps despair at bay;
all is not lost.

Our lot must be cast again,
our bread spread upon the waters.
We may be driven down or not,
or not forever,
unventured forth we will never know,
colors struck without a fight.

Do not be taken so easily,
held hostage by the past,
life surrendered before it is due.
Hold fast to what is held dear,
take the chance,
accept the risk,
try, try again.

You are not alone.
We all fight the jaded beast.

—July 2011

84.

The word "but" lands a heavy blow. It is readily at hand when we say we will act but do not mean now, when we consider doing something but are not sure, when praise is deserved but not too much, when we want to keep someone close but not too near. It buys time and hedges committing. What is to be read into this word "but"? If too much, a future may be foreclosed. If too little, delusion may go on too long. These are difficult questions.

But

"But" is a fearsome word,
something good rarely follows,
taking away with the other hand
what it gives,
diminishing what it meant,
emptying its words,
sincerity gone,
no longer pretense.
No praise can survive it;
no compliment can remain alive,
better left unsaid all that is left.

Why could you not hold it?
Why say anything if you
could not spare it?
Nothing else will be heard,
its landing hard,
worsening insecurities and doubt,
staggering next steps.

Where is the shaken soul to turn?
Who to believe in now?
How much will be set adrift
by but's release?

—March 2019

85.

It is said we are what we do. Are we? How much is to satisfy the demands of others? This is not an idle inquiry. It goes to the heart of who we are. Is this truly us or only an interim pause? Do we have a sense of self apart from the motions of life we go through—the real us, so to speak? Do we ever say, "This isn't me"? Who, then, is it? These questions look to our identity, our values, our goals, and the compromises we tell ourselves we must make to get there. Have the concessions been too much? Gone on too long? Has one corner too many been cut? We should ask before it is too late.

The Summons

Life summons us with its tugs and pulls,
its claims of ownership as if entitled,
demanding on its terms,
the price of admission if we want to play.
What else can we do?

Something within resists,
unwilling to surrender all.
And so begin the clever efforts
to convince ourselves it is not forever,
we will get back to knowing better
that somehow never comes,
always one more thing
on the road to later.

But the unrest goes on;
it knows us best.
We have a summoning of our own,
our inner self calling us to return.

We can feel it,
asking where a stand will be made
and when.
Do we know?
Will bided time arrive
before it runs out?

—June 2011

86.

Secrets. We all have them, ours and those we keep for others. They steal from us without our knowing, their grip rarely relaxing on its own. But time is not on their side. They will be found out. What if they are not? Are we the worse for it? Are those for whom they are kept? Are they hidden acts of kindness sparing others or calculated choices saving us? Are we better off if the secrets forever obscure what is true? What kind of unreal world do we live in then? What have the secrets taken from us?

Secrets

Secrets have a life of their own,
controlling with orders not to tell
and threats if we do.
Fear is a ruthless stalker,
not required to carry through,
its warnings enough to do its work,
presenting a picture not real,
leading others into an altered world
of us,
askew in ways not seen.

It is a struggle,
this keeping inside,
the masquerade of no one knowing.
Ours are burden enough—
what more do we carry for others?
Are we benevolent sparers of pain?
Coward keepers afraid of being seen?
Conscripted knowers unwilling to reveal?
What a toll the hiding takes!

What is better? What is worse?
The price paid for the secrets we reveal
or the draining weight of the untold.
Which will it be?
We alone with our secrets,
or returned to the world behind them
as it truly is.

—June 2010

87.

We would be the first to deny a belief in magic. Yet there is evidence to the contrary. We see this in the insistence "It will all work out" with no thought or plan, or "We'll figure it out" with no idea when or how. "Later" may make its appearance—"I'll deal with this later"—or the waiting game of doing nothing. But the impending cannot be escaped so easily. Consequences will come collecting either way.

Magic

We believe in magic
more than we know or dare admit,
going by many names,
blind belief not able to withstand
the slightest look,
the "somehow" sleight of thought—
things will get better,
it will work out,
we'll figure it out
somehow—
as if the answer will spring forth
on its own,
a retreat into later that never comes
or comes too late,
clinging to denial when the happening
has passed the point of no return,
pretending the threatening future
will never arrive
with gathering waves at the shore.

But the Coming is on its way
clearing magic as it goes;

it comes for us,
reckoning will have its day.
So have your magic for a while
if you must,
we all do,
but know there are limits.

—November 2007

88.

Mistakes. We all make them. What sway do they have? Do we learn and go on? Or stay mired in second-guessing and self-pity leaving us timid and afraid? Mistakes are next steps to next choices. We must face them, not with doubt and hesitation, but with confidence from where we have been.

Mistakes

Mistakes,
I do not welcome you,
will resist you to the end,
but when you come for me
as you will,
let me learn from you.
Is that your purpose,
more benign than you seem?
Without you, is there nothing to learn?

Why tempt me with doubt,
fear of wrong again,
forcing hesitation and worry,
second-guessing the next deed done
until you render judgment?
Could you not find another way?

How soon will you approach?
Can you have a gentler touch
if I promise to learn faster?
I will wait for you,
look for signs you are near,

schooled with what I have learned,
not knowing when you will arrive,
just that you will.

—August 2009

89.

Battle lines are drawn everywhere in the culture wars of today. Differences have been weaponized. The question "Why?" has joined the partisan fray. We see it when asked why we believe this or think that when no reasons will be good enough for a mind made up. The query, innocent as it may seem, is put forth as a challenge, an opening salvo in the argument to come. Just as potent and feigning equal sincerity is the seeming invitation "Explain to me," when no explanation is needed or will do, its dismissal at the ready. How to respond? We must put a marker down for the truth, for the facts, knowing they will not convince. We must not let the question go unanswered as if we have no response.

The Why Weapon

What a life "why" has,
passing for wanting to know,
it soon has designs of its own
as we learn its many uses—
sometimes buying time,
other times passing for curiosity,
even interest,
polite if nothing else,
but only one question deep,
bracing for the unwanted answer,
already on to the next.

It can be pointed,
masking the challenge to what is asked,
straw man for the argument to come,
not so neutral as it is seems,
clear to those who know its provenance,

defenses are raised,
no answer will do—
the "why" has said it all.

And so we return to our corners,
less willing to provide an answer
not really wanted
to a question not really asked.

—January 2019

90.

Sometimes we are at a loss for words. A death, a funeral, a crushing illness, tragic news. We want to say something, but what? We have the best of intentions. Not knowing how to get our feelings out, not wanting to make the hurt worse, and not wanting to minimize, we may settle for a platitude as safe, or at least less wrong, and take our awkward leave feeling we should have said more.

No Words

Words can fail us
when we need them most.
So much felt,
so much needing saying,
so much wanting to say,
but beyond our reach,
the words put off by aching silence
and we,
grateful for the simplest platitude
to fall back on,
anything but nothing,
grateful it was not us.

Will the words come in time?
Too late,
it was time we did not have,
the painful hush worsening as it goes.
They are there, the words,
we can feel them
but they will not form.
Let them out who holds them back!

We are left with feelings
we could not express,
sorry for the little we had to say,
failing them just as the words fail us,
sure we have learned and will do better
but somehow never do,
fearing it could be us,
guilty it was not
as if we have no right,
we have done nothing
but nor did they,
and we wonder and are lost
not knowing why.

—February 2018

91.

On a lighter note, a word should be said about something we all know well: the waiting room at the doctor's office. There, time comes to a halt. Every visit begins the same—in the waiting room. Upon entering, we surrender our outside lives. What we have to do does not matter. Our time is of no consequence. If we have somewhere else to be, no concern for those here. We count for nothing, nameless, faceless. We are made to feel we should be grateful for the appointment at all. One day in the waiting room, I dutifully took my place and—surprise!—had time enough to write this.

The Waiting Room

The waiting room
hangs heavy with defeat.
Time has stopped;
not even the big hand moves,
people with everywhere
and nowhere to go
the same,
slowed and halted by the relentless wait
to be called,
only to face another room,
put on hold again,
grateful even for that.
Time has no value for those out here,
and so it goes until we emerge;
the time warp has ended,
time resumes,
free at last.

—September 1998

92.

In the waiting room again. This day, I observed a tentative approach to the receptionist and heard those hopeful words: "I have an appointment." I watched as the appointment book was scanned in vain for some sign this was so. Then the look of alarm as the receptionist solemnly declared for all to hear, "I don't have you in my book." Next, the pleading voice, "But I made the appointment. I must be in there. Can you look again?" The sparring went on for several rounds until the bout ended with, "I'm sorry. I don't have you in my book." I was thankful it was not me.

The Appointment Book

"I'm here for my appointment,"
he said.

"Let me see.
I don't have you in my book."

"But I called, and they told me to come.
They would take care of it," he said.

"I don't have you in my book."

"But I spoke with them,
not with a book;
they said they would put me down.
I'm here just as they told me."

"I'm sorry,
I don't have you in my book."

"I don't care about your book;
it doesn't mean I didn't call
and wasn't told to come.
Your book is not my doing,
not my fault.
I called—
it's all I could do—
and I'm here."

"I'm sorry,
there's nothing I can do.
I don't have you in my book."

"And what of my book?
I have a book too.
It's called my life.
My time is worth something.
Does anyone have me in their book?"

And then the doleful retreat,
slow backing away,
knowing this was overheard,
knowing it would be said
and heard again.

—September 1998

93.

What next? Tomorrow? The day after? We count on them being here. We plan for their coming. Why would we not? We must live, not as if there is no tomorrow, but as if there is. We know we could end in an instant. Until that moment, we are in the ongoing Now with time for all our minds can see. Where will it take us? Where will we go? Wherever we choose.

Next

Next,
what life ahead
do you hold for me?
What twists and turns to get there?
Are my choices fewer
with not as far to go?
Do they mean more with less space
for being wrong?
Will my learnings from your past
be enough?
There is always more to know;
the dice always roll.
I need no answers,
just that you appear another day
and the next.
I will do the rest.

—April 2019

Epilogue

How to end this winding journey through these pages? With thanks. For what? For the freedom of having choices, not forced into living the lives of others. For the kindness of time and its harsh lessons. They teach us relentlessly, and we have much to learn. For the inspiration we feel from lyrics and prose, from poetic depths and transcendent highs. For the introspection we might never have reached without disappointment and loss. They give us much to think about and ready us to go on. And for the joy—the sheer joy—of unscripted thoughts that burst upon us with their beauty and laughter. What a lesser world it would be without them!

Where to from here? We will have a say, but not the final word. Life, time, and happenstance will see to that. Will there be forks in the road ahead? Of course. Even now they are on their way. But it is these twists and turns that draw the best from us and allow us to give life meaning.